Orjuana Khudari, a poet at heart from a young age and a surgeon-under-training, journeying and learning from life encounters, with surgery and poetry as company.

for those who, despite everything, choose to hold on.

Orjuana Khudari

SUTURED INTO PLACE

AUSTIN MACAULEY PUBLISHERS™

LONDON • CAMBRIDGE • NEW YORK • SHARJAH

ISBN – 9789948793588 – (Paperback)
ISBN – 9789948793595 – (E-Book)

Application Number: MC-10-01-2081902
Age Classification: E

Printer Name: iPrint Global Ltd
Printer Address: Witchford, England

First Published 2023
AUSTIN MACAULEY PUBLISHERS FZE
Sharjah Publishing City
P.O Box [519201]
Sharjah, UAE
www.austinmacauley.ae
+971 655 95 202

I'd like to acknowledge the continuous love and support provided by my parents, siblings, family and friends.

I'd like to thank the life I've lived so far with all the experiences I went through, by choice or force, the good and bad, the hurt and growth; for building me into what I became and wrote this with. Not everything is of personal experience, yet written with empathy.

My final thank you is to you, for holding on, for looking for growth despite all, for reading the words my heart wrote. Thank you.

Table of Contents

sutured into place,
despite all the cuts and falls,
despite the closed ends and walls;
here's growth into grace.

Cuts and Falls

to me, the grief for those i lost is small
but grief of loss itself hurts more;
we'll meet others along the line, after all.

but recollecting oneself after a loss
may happen as slowly as a crawl,
since with every loss
a part of us falls off.
so
nobody's crying over your loss,
they're most likely farewell-ing
the part they no longer own
and constructively repairing
their flesh and bone.

we wake up each day
hoping to feel less weight on our shoulder,
thinking we finally passed yesterday.
but we find ourselves carrying another
load of weight for the future;
living life with a worry for each matter.

yet the fault isn't in our past encounters
but a deeply hidden terror
of what lays ahead
and what may occur;
we fear the unknown
and fear falling into error.

sometimes i sit and wonder,
what makes these days so cold?
is it the fantasies we build
or the dreams we hold,
when reality strikes,
shatter us most?

there are two types of rocks;
few that we can lean on
and others that tightly hold on
to us
to shrink us to the bottom.
not everyone's worth trusting,
never let that slip you nor be forgotten.

i guess i aimed too high,
thought i'd achieve more
and as far as my eyes
wandered away from shore.
i know and i won't deny
how broken i feel right now
but i won't let my hope die;
i'll get there.
i was just not ready then.

creating art isn't as beautiful as art itself is.
enjoying this art is different to how creating it feels;
there's pain of six feet under ground
instead of cloud nine bliss.
there's so much behind these creations,
more than poetry reveals.
there's tiredness of crying after every fall,
tiredness of falling after every rise,
tiredness of growing, then breaking again
to pieces that are far too small.
but that's how art is written on the wall.

with every breakdown poets create art;
turning what felt like an end of the path into poetry.
similarly, when a poet's soul is breaking apart
the result is an artistic creation
as they try to mend their heart.

if only these creations were collected,
hanged on walls of museums, treasured
and remembered throughout history
for how they can touch one's heart from afar;
like a framed untouchable enthralling beauty.

poetic art is only words written in solitary;
though beautiful and a sign of bravery.
because survival makes the most
beautiful pieces of art.
even if temporary; for we'll fall again
and the cycle will restart.

our world is one of uncertainty
where not all matters are under your control,
unlike games of chess with their kings, queens
and knights that protect you from harm by any means.

it's one where people hide their unbearable schemes
under masks of deceiving faces
like those pictured on magazines.
it's a world where people come and go
and even those you thought
you'd never lose down the stream;
you'd wake up one day
and find they've either become a foe
or gone and nowhere to be seen.

yet if losing someone occurred easily,
they're not worth moaning over;
another gain would be by just another corner.

so let the world pass you by,
get over those who leave you to die
and only hold on
to those holding onto you,
for the world has seven billion
others that we could connect with too.

i can feel it, i can feel their flow;
their current had never been stronger before.
these flashbacks are close to knocking me out;
although they're fragments of good memories
that onto each other, trying to, mount.

that's the funny thing about memories;
the good can release a few tears
even if they were happy and safe,
like a once pretty painting now smudged
as pain against them smears.
yet i'd rather have smears of pain,
than smears that ruin the picture
and erase the memory from my brain.

what have we become
without each other?
so different compared to the plans
we planned to achieve together.
what happened to us?
my heart's about to shatter.

sometimes feelings are caught
but mostly they're fought
back down to non-existence.
the heartless became the sought
and the heartfelt; the fraud.

weren't we once a complex
that followed one another's progress
to make sure life's okay
as we built each other's wings?
then why'd we fly away
outside each other's rings?
out of reach today
and never seen again the following springs;
using what i helped you with
to fly away and break our strings.

won't we like to be blinded by brightness
without the existence of such harshness
clouding us into darkness,
but to be surrounded by all things harmless?

won't we like our high hopes to not fall down,
to not witness faces walking with a frown
in every corner of our town?

won't we like to live through a moment
where we'd know love is born?
won't we like to be in love to the point,
apart from that person, we cannot be torn?
won't we like to have beautiful friendships
that support one another's missing half
and where our remedy is to hear the other laugh.

won't we like to be able to see
without all these blurry lines?
won't we like to be able to hear
without these constant whines?

won't we like to drown into a sea of peace
where all is ordered neatly with no crease,
where our world is just one big masterpiece.

can our likes and wishes be granted?
can a wish factory exist?
can our dreams come true
no matter how long is our list?

we simply wish to live overjoyed
in a world so content with nothing destroyed.
begin by you
and a change will follow.

if you don't love for me
what you love for yourself,
i'm afraid we can no longer be,
nor can we call this love.

once i felt it all slip away,
small pieces every day.
until a broken world
was all that surrounded me.
i tried to flee,
but no success.
i tried to run,
but my legs won't budge.

all was broken,
nothing was working.

but no matter how hard we break,
or how small the broken pieces of us become;
none of this is the end.
there's no doubt we can, eventually, mend.
even if everything is no longer one
or the same size
but shattered pieces all across;
there's still a chance to rise.

deep breath after another,
i told myself to not let the pain bother
neither i nor my hope
for it's all i had to cope.

one step at a time
was all i did to climb
and shoo all negativity away
as if it were a big roaming fly.

i then managed to get my tears dry
to clearly see the sky
and we rose;
the no longer broken world and i.

some are temporary,
not everyone lasts
to create history
of filling our future and past.

how do people so openly, on each other, hate?
how do they think it's just
an opinion they're trying to state?
there's a difference between having an opinion
and reaching out to another person's locked gate
to force your hate onto them aiming to break
the homey feeling they built
as they grew comfortable under their skin.
how could one not hesitate
when they are about to create
a so-called opinion that wouldn't tolerate
how the recipient would feel.

we're all different
and may like things that are miles apart,
one can easily and silently depart
without bashing out hate
on what doesn't seem to be their taste,
as we don't have to be alike.

i'm just me;
imperfect the way i am
and just like the sea
sometimes calm,
other times a mess of waves.

sometimes we forget the memories
we want to remember.
other times, we remember the memories
we want to forget.
they may catch us off guard and when we're tender,
bringing, at times, past pain and renewed regret.

while the forgotten that we'd like to keep,
could just be hidden and buried too deep;
they may only visit us during sleep,
to evaporate the minute we wake up.

if we already know such things don't last,
shouldn't we have not gotten attached from the start?
or is it inescapable; how they can fool a heart.

lost my balance and noticed a little sway,
wondered where was i heading and why astray?
didn't want to back down nor run, hide or be tucked away.

i hoped to continue down the road without being the prey
of all these mistakes that were here to delay
reaching my destination without betray.

they may have broken my heart
and caused my strength to slip away,
but i know i should hide all breakage from display,
regain my strength before i'm drowned in dismay.

i'll learn to walk through and find my passageway,
i'll hold on to the little strength i still have overlay
in hope to bloom
and protect my petals to never decay.

grieving the living
is painful too,
they're still around,
but no longer for you.

motional world;
people come and go
and some
were only here for show.

Closed Ends and Walls

they lie to us with phrases
like "everything will get back to normal"
but life keeps moving on and pages
turn as stories try to complete.

"things will get back to how they were"
but what kind of life goes on repeat?
there's a reaction to every action
and even with words, there's no retraction.

yet all i hope is what we were isn't broken
because of something neither of us did
but an effect of our surroundings.
i know we can't, in time, go back
and smoothness may lack this rebounding.
but i'd hate to see our story reach a black
dead-end already
than continue on with a healed crack.

remember when we loved the sea
and how the wind made us feel free?
remember when we thought waves were fun;
we stood against them without protection?
little did we know, as little rocks, we'd be overrun
by the sea waves to the point of separation
into two different directions.
we were sent off and away, far too early.
i, to leave behind what we had, wasn't yet ready;
we had so many plans and a half made journey.
but i was here and you, a number
i forced myself not to remember
of miles away.

sometimes, i feel your absence
and hope to run into you in shock;
we travelled and went against the flow of waves.
but you settled down and found another rock;
another to accompany you in dark caves.

let's not make promises
we may break under the pressure of falling rain.
they may keep others as hostages
holding onto a promise as if by a chain.
waiting, even past delays,
to only be greeted by pain.

life's already a long journey of possible sways;
broken promises will only hold back a moving train.

maybe it's because we spend our time
looking forward to endings
good or bad, both a climb,
before actually climbing.

maybe it's because we envision
endings of our own making
before things have even begun.

maybe because of actions such as these,
we find ourselves only at endings;
every corner a locked door with no keys,
for we are living less
than we do grieve
for every incomplete reach.

even if forgiveness was provided,
feelings don't ignite twice.
what follows would mostly be one-sided;
once gone, no price
can buy them back again.

we've allowed nonsense to fill our thoughts
without feeling their faults.
we're feeding on the littleness of this world
unaware that we may become empty vaults.

but can't you see?
all these meaningless conversations,
but-ins and arguments,
they're drifting us to the blue;
to what we clouded ourselves
to believe is a beautiful mesmerising view,
but it's all a mess.

your eyes
held my free heart
hostage with ties
to never part.

i turned around a couple of times
and always found you standing there,
although i hardly answer your asking eyes
but prefer to keep myself out of share;
you stayed and showed me your care.

till i, with time, began to slowly unravel
and with you, life became easier to handle.

yet i fear a future
where you'll become my essential
dose of water.

you drew the gap
and i let it trap
me on one side,
you on the other
side of the map.

even friends
are becoming trends;
their decision to stay now depends
on the situation at hand.
maybe if they become for rent,
we can actually extend
their stay and delay the end.

don't rush in trustfully;
not everyone holds the intent
to stay a friend
or love purely without minusing a percent.
if newcomers come along,
proceed superficially first and don't bend
so another loss
doesn't become another lesson learnt.

if i knew characters of my unfinished stories
and you and i would share the same fate;
i would've forced myself to write them an end
for you and i, to get the chance, to complete.

we're never the same old self we once were.
with time, we change and grow.
so when there's distance in between
we no longer fully, the other person, know.

even if it's just a small detail or a new habit,
it's not the same as how it was before.
feels like we're towards each other; offshore.

a thin line; might be unseen
had created a gap and drew us apart.
i wonder, is this how endings start?

i think of almost and i remember you.
i think of wishing and i see you.
i think of reaching out
and i touch a blank space empty of you.

we're all humans that feel
and have words of opinion to speak.
no person has the right to seal
another's voice or assume it's weak.
everyone deserves to be heard
and given a chance to prove wrongs.

to be unvoiced hurts
and would only create broken songs,
instead of an outcome that'd be much preferred
where the unvoiced is no longer but where it belongs
creating wonders that would be in history remembered;
if only given the chance.

i can't re-love you again
after you made me un-love you for a while.
recreating feelings isn't a piece of cake
nor am i one to fake
to satisfy your drive of over a mile
back to me, even if past a hurricane.

within the corners of my mind,
thoughts make perfect sense.
i can easily think and find
words of satisfaction, no less.

but as if i turn, to what's in me, blind;
i struggle whenever i try to outwardly express
thoughts that were once aligned
as they become a complete mess,
that i can't fix nor pull forward from behind
a curtain of blindness.

aren't we all, under the surface,
trying to find our lives' purpose?
aren't we all, behind the mask,
hiding parts of us as if it's a required task?
aren't we all, more than what's already out there,
have plenty of us to share?
aren't we all, without our facade,
scared to face the world and afraid?

but if we are all the same
then why are we playing this game?
why can't we be ourselves without shame,
without having to, our quirkiness, tame?

i am me and you are you;
we are free
to be who we'd like to be.

in this world, there are no eternities,
unending time is one of our inabilities;
that's how we became strangers
with memories.

i know our last goodbye was a while ago,
but haven't you thought of how it'd go
if we were to have another hello?

would our heartbeats race or slow?
would we still have that same ol' glow?
would our conversations, as before, smoothly flow?

it's not less painful for those who leave
than those who stay behind;
neither move on with ease.

how long do we have until all bright sides end?
can we always look
on the bright side of something and depend
on it to make things better,
won't their number descend?
won't all our surroundings
turn black eventually once they end?
once we, of bright sides, run out
for how many times we've used them
repeatedly and throughout
hurt, pain, loss and doubt.

would we always have their company?
doesn't it sound impossible?
'cause it does to me.

i only hope whenever this blackness comes
i won't be overtaken suddenly;
i won't turn around and find nothingness welcoming me.

how does one live
in a world with such width,
without knights of a chess game
to move diagonally with.

you never know
what people hold in their inner core,
or any of what they have in store,
nor when they'll let it out of the door,
or how many layers, to secure it, they wore,
nor do you have to, the unknown, adore.
but simply don't judge a book by its cover.

don't break the little that we have
and then wait for me to chase after you.
i can move on, already started to.
we weren't close enough to begin with,
for this breakage to feel like falling from a cliff.

i didn't fall;
i awaked away,
i know my worth
and when to stay.

Growth

don't ask me how'd i get that scar
but what, in the healing process, have i learnt?
what it helped me add to my secret jar
and how have i, with its burning pain, dealt?

don't ask me what's wrong
but what have i collected from what went under?
and how will i make it into a new lifelong
motto to live by and not re-suffer?

don't ask me why some writings turn into sad songs
but what did i manage to buffer
as a lesson learnt out of every rupture
that life aims and blows?

only then, with each answer, would you be helping me
plant my seeds and strengthen my growth.
otherwise, it's pointless talk over tea
without new extracts to cook over the stove
nor add to the jar of lessons of how to live and be.

it's okay to tear up
for what almost was
but never became
other than wishes
burnt into flame.

but venture to dry up,
build yourself once more
to help you reclaim
the life ahead of you
to reign.

i still have some of who you were
with me, embedded as my own.
souls take from each other as time goes by
and i guess what you gave me wasn't for loan.
life changed and we parted ways,
yet parts of you haven't left me alone.

although you no longer occupy my side,
what you left on my flesh and bone
aren't leftovers i regret
as each has already made themselves at home;
we live and learn to become a combination
made of more than one type of stone.

despite losing people at times, keep standing
with open arms for whatever will be, your way, thrown.
welcome a better combination, of everything
learnt and experienced, to call your own.

while drops of falling rain, unlike snow,
could reflect colours against the gloominess;
people falling does not sequel the same show.

there's no beauty in a human fall
without a rise, even if the process was slow.
but what keeps us fallen in stillness
is the poison we let flow
in our system and past our walls' thickness
that we once dedicated ourselves to grow;
was lost as the impulse
of giving up stroke us while we're feeling low.

but who's to say there's an end to our limits?
we could be the poison's antidote
if we were to devote
ourselves to not only rise but float
and cough out the poison to empty our throat.

we could float above waves
instead of lie between graves;
ahead of us are plenty of unknown days.

you're not the canvas of the sail,
giver of chances to those who fail
at loyalty or such tale.
be the sailboat itself
and give no third chances
to those undeserving and impure,
rather leave them behind and sail away;
give yourself a chance to enjoy the tour.

live and learn
to forgive yourself
for all the things you yearned
but didn't become.
learn to congratulate your spine
for holding more stories
than books can and still be fine.

light may not be visible at the tunnel
when you're not near the end,
with no more energy to spend.
a breath may not be easy to take
when you're not close to the surface
and almost out of purpose.

but it's end-results we work out for;
to get off every fall and floor,
even if every end is another shore.
if not infinite waves that we ride,
what kind of gain would life provide?

so fight and hold on, day and night;
it's how we become individuals
we hold for, much pride.

without excruciating experiences,
joys of achievement won't be felt
or even known.
only with different voltages,
of highs and lows,
would art really be born,
so keep holding on.

i'm working on me for me;
proving all assumptions wrong,
peeling off my weakened self, step by step
to reveal my strength, for i need to be strong.

i'll be ready for the bricks and walls i'll face,
i know the road i sat on taking is long,
but i'm here, with an already done shoe lace,
and along the way,
i'll stand by the values that to me, belong.

don't dare become a candle
that burns itself without thought
in order to handle
other people's darkness and fault,
to help them while you fade
in an empty uncared for vault.
light your own pathway and be your own aid;
not everyone we burn out for
joins our darkness and doesn't leave us behind, betrayed.

while falls may leave permanent scars;
every lesson learnt from each
would not only light your way with stars
but draw wrinkles of growth
on your once young soul, as it rose.

every sunrise brings another day,
having the worst past
doesn't mean you get to stay
in the same track.
you can still find your way
and create your very own desired future.

we don't have to part ways,
nor do you have to go
to wander and learn how to grow,
i won't stop your flow.
i'm unfinished too and yet to glow;
we can discover and grow as we go,
accompany each other on the low,
protect one another against the blow
and walk until we're on the front row.

we can change and become
all that we want despite the rain and snow;
without untying us,
without the loss,
but with love.

it's not a straightforward path,
but filled with falls, holes and scars.
if we looked forward to the aftermath
and planted seeds on dirt after wars,
we might see results better than ash.

if instead of closing doors with force,
we welcomed our chosen ones with warmth,
maybe they'd water our seeds
and we'd flower forth.

if hearts weren't so blind
by the surface of others
and instead dined
with whom they like
to know what kind of mind
people grew behind
all of their charade,
maybe then
hearts won't be played
and minds would grow to respect
one another enough to last a decade;
followed by nothing less but a direct
motion of love that isn't even delayed
but in perfect timing.

we weren't made to be immortal nor unbreakable;
sometimes we stumble and become broken shards
scattered across the widest of yards.
other times we're puzzling ourselves together;
each time a different puzzle of art.

don't blame the broken road
for you going astray;
it's all a test for you to find your way.
it's not wrong to sway
if we learn and continue living
without repetition of yesterday.

even those who seem as hard as stone
may only be putting on a mask;
some have grown extremely prone
to slipping signs of anything other than
emotions expected to be shown.
yet even stones, if specifically handled right,
can fire up, not only an entire zone
but a whole forest ablaze.

study a person with patience
to know what gets them drawn
if you'd like to intervene
between what's faked by a mask
and what to their heart is real.

over time some perceptions change
and willingly or not we could no longer feel the same
to those around us when we uncover their dressed up lies,
once standing in a picture perfect frame.
with wide open eyes
past feelings can drain
down the sink and demise.

it's okay
to walk away.

too often do we fall apart,
too often do we think it's beyond repair,
the damage that put us in despair.
but if all we did was stay up the chart
and life didn't, every now
and then, push us down;
we'd just be following the flow
with hardly any "i think i've grown."

you are not, of anyone else's love, in desperate need.
love of yourself by you, is what you should on, feed.
water yourself with self-love; until your seed
is no longer but an already grown tree that is guaranteed
to hold you up whenever you're about to bleed.

a grown tree of self-love, blooming all year round,
is the beginning of our need.
only then, once that is achieved
do we fall in love with another and be loved.
the extra love that will, in turn, be received;
will be like a cherry on top.

every single part of us is fragile;
our heart, our mind with our thoughts and opinions,
those are merely a small example.
fragility could break us today or tomorrow;
it's a constant endless battle.
no matter how many we pass, millions
will appear, and our tract, follow.

that's why we build walls to eventually create a castle.
you might think they'll eat me alive, but they only swallow
attacks sent my way to protect me while i travel
and grow day by day with less sorrow.
our castles minimise our fragility
and strengthen us by blocking any existent hollows
on confidence, self-esteem and creativity.

though castles are full of windows and doors
so we mustn't forget to include them when buildin'
they might be considered as leakage-causing pores;
but we need them to not let these walls lock us in.
ending up with windows for beauty escapes
and walls of force.

perfection is out of the realms of possibilities
for we fall and struggle,
we make mistakes and give apologies,
we fall, occasionally, in and out of trouble.
but once, from our falls, we learn;
repetition won't be a concern.

yet life is short and we're bound
to fall more times than we'd like
and so observing what goes around
to learn from other's mistakes
is the way to live in the battleground.

aim to win over your demons
before you let someone walk into your mind;
some people own their lover's demons
to save them, out of love, blind.
don't be the cause of such harm and evil
to those you should be most kind.

if your mistake is already made,
don't leave the lover and demons behind;
you caused the change of shade
that coloured them into something else out of mind,
it's only right to offer aid
and win over the demons together.

despite the wilderness and it's danger,
one can live if were braver.
plus bravery's best feature
is that even a little can be enough;
for it'll grow, with time, on itself
making the once dry wilderness greener.

i was once different
changed by many alterations
that life kept throwing my way,
for i've swam through moving waters
and drowned sometimes, yet didn't still lay.
i've weathered unstable weathers
to stabilise myself and not sway.
i managed to cross many borders
in hope to become what i envisioned, if i may.
in between, i tried to not give in to pressures
but fought storms along the way.

i know it isn't the end and this is part of the venture;
i didn't reach where i reached today
to let strikes of lightning cause forest fires
and leave me as a burning ember.

i still have desires
to keep going, though right now tender,
but i'll figure a way to get up again,
for i am a fighter.

you and i own different shoes
and look out from different window views,
we're also made up of dissimilar screws
and a core unlike another among these queues.

our differences could bring us together like magnets
or draw us apart in a chaotic madness;
the cause of such is an absence
of understanding each other's personalities.

but we all live on one earth
and no difference between us is worth
such divisions of destruction;
all it takes is extra awareness and acceptance.

some streams are uneven,
some falls are part of journeying,
but you won't drown by falling
in the water;
you'll drown by staying
right there.

we may've felt empty at times
with a need to have some spaces filled.
but the fault is not a missing piece
that someone else held;
it's on us to draw the lines
and our structure, by ourselves, build.

the road will not even,
whether at the beginning or halfway through.
this walk is not easing,
nor would it help if you were to change a shoe.
but those who believed in reaching
and have taken every lesson along the way;
confidence can be seen defining their steps
not because the road has finally even,
but because they can now walk on
what they previously tripped over.

hold your doors open;
any walkouts are welcome to leave.
have no intention to retrieve
hearts that broke relations
for worthless reasons.

it's humanly typical for such encounters to hurt;
the walls we're building are still young
and unseen pains can still burst
through without notice, till late.
some can be avoided and curved,
while others can pass through us straight.
despite all the difference in severity and rate;
all could build our strength,
if we keep choosing to hold on.

learn to ride waves
or you'll break as you collide
and underneath them slide;
drowning.

nothing comes at ease,
nor does the result of hardship cease.
hold on and pull a few all-nighters
for a better tomorrow;
we happen to have hearts of fighters
that aim to blow away yesterday's sorrow.

it's not goodbye once the sun sets
even through the darkness; a moon's light could fit
to extract wonders from each of us
and force these haunted candles to lit.

we're full of aims of change and improvement
without a hesitation to begin our movement
of forward steps for our future's empowerment.

you're not broken
these are only bruises;
don't lose yourself down this road,
but attempt to rise above the abusers
and set some act into motion.

we seem to count the candles on the cake
each birthday as we celebrate
as a way to count the years we've lived
and advertise our growth.
although that's fine, but alone it's not enough;
growth nor maturity are measured by age.

but by how many times you've broken out
of your comfort zone's cage,
how much experience you've survived
how many to-dos' have you ticked off the page,
how much of what life taught you have you utilised,
and much more that's more revealing of growth
than the number of candles one blows.

i remember wanting to set a date
with happiness to meet and greet
and maybe get acquainted and appreciate
the desire i long wished to seek.
but time seemed to continuously leak
out of my reach, and my calendar reeked
of things to do and meet,
filled with everything but happiness for years.

until i realised happiness is not waited upon
but created and made in-between life and careers
lived and won
anytime one wished with no date to set.

to create oneself alone

is art

and a journey to discover the unknown

without regard

to obstacles, against us, thrown.

stars may never align,
the world may never fully unite,
the sun won't always shine;
there are many impossibilities
but communicating well enough
shouldn't be one of them.
for such ability isn't tough
if we were to listen
instead of hmm
and if we allowed our vision
to study what's hidden;
we'll understand those around us.

one must learn to stand on their own feet
and look into the world with their own eyes
to create their own flow and beat;
instead of being carried away by waves
created by the views of everyone they meet.

wherever we are
for whatever different purpose;
encounters don't go far
if our first impression
didn't turn out well but bizarre.

we must learn how to present ourself
neatly with our best aspects
on the front shelf
while hide the rest up the attics;
as we can't go on talking about everything we did
only emphasise on key points with italics
and let the rest of our work speak of us.

we're each our own person
and our difference is our key
whether others like it or dislike it,
it shouldn't be
of our concern,
for we don't have to be everyone's cup of tea;
just be you and i'll be me.

once, twice or more times in our lives
we must've felt guilty,
though as the feeling consumes us, we lay unaware
of how we may have control
over how we proceed from there.
this guilt may drown us fair and square,
or it may give us purpose
to not allow the feeling's recurrence,
to make better decisions and choices.

it's all up to us, what type of guilt we'd like ours to be;
a burden that slowly eats us alive,
or a purpose that helps us, for better, strive.
a purpose that, with all the consuming guilt,
would push us to survive.

we're more than the little others know of us;
we're more than we know ourselves yet.
so don't draw a full picture with your brush
when the picture is not even whole yet.
no matter how long it has been since we met
one cannot draw a picture of another
that could be a complete fit.

i might've drowned in the deep blue sea
or lost parts of me in life's hurricane
as i hesitated to surrender at its mercy.
it might've drifted me slightly off my lane,
i might've, once or twice, scratched my knee.

but between the curtains of falling rain
and from the bottom of the sea
or a ground that's full of mud and dirt;
i have emerged before over the pain.

there isn't an end of ups, downs and hurt,
there's no promise that i won't fall again.
but i have the heart of a young bird
still learning to fly without a holding-back chain.

there's more of me that i don't know,
sides that i haven't yet seen.
is it more time that i need?
or do i simply have to dig deep?
or both combined, for i, to be found.
found by me, to be known by me.

with every incident i seem to explore
colours that light could refract furthermore
to what is me, and what to me is a bore,
to what i don't like and would rather change.
since we're not entitled to stick to who we become;
modifying one's self to the better, isn't strange.

it's an on-going process of discovery;
a journey with little painted outcomes
for i, to create my own gallery.
a gallery filled with what makes me, me.
for only i to enjoy and see; an owned property.

and even then, surrounded by all that beauty
i would still not fully know me.
them, you and i each are a captivating mystery.

ease doesn't build us,
hardship does.
it's not a journey
with only forward steps
but also some failed attempts.
nobody gets anywhere
sleeping all day on their beds;
fight for what you want and don't declare
the white flag of giving up.

i can be me
without you,
for i've always been me,
before you.

there will never be two people
with the same way of thinking, even lovers.
there has to be varieties, but we can't let that divide us,
since every thought matters.
only aim to change thoughts that may bring harm
and simply leave the others.

because varieties paint a picture
filled with different colours.

me, myself and i
will never be parted,
will never have to say goodbye.

as one, this life we started
and still going strong, is our tie.
too strong to be destructed,
too strong to one day die.

i promised to not take me for granted
because no one else can occupy
the place of me in my heart.

although, i like having others nearby;
they may complete, of my life, a part
and sometimes i can, on them, rely.

but without me, i would be long gone underlie.

twenty eighteen
was a rich seasonal year,
felt and lived with the most sincere
of ups, downs and in-between.

roads may not have been clear,
mistakes often did interfere,
but no progress comes from a dull routine.
so despite dark nights of fear,
we walked ahead, none settled at the rear,
no matter how tempting was the scene.

other nights, stars reached out so near
to help guide new decisions and clear
paths to face the unseen.
even winter storms couldn't steer
goals out of focus nor ruin the atmosphere;
for the end must be spring green.

regardless of continuous thunder
and all the obstacles we had to suffer,
we used them to fuel up, as gasoline.

even under pressure and the heat of summer,
every life lesson taught us how to recover
past the pain without having to lean,
longer than necessary, on another shoulder.

still at times, like fall leaves, we fall and shatter,
break and detach all strings,
close-up on ourselves and cluster.
but with patience, rain will follow to water
the wounded and help regain
our strength to blossom for spring.

despite the struggles, we can buffer
moments tinted with the brightest of colours
that fill our hearts of songs to sing
as we celebrate an achiever
and, in reaching dreams, a true believer.

such ups may seem temporary; for we'll fall again
and the cycle will restart.
but ongoing journeys of survival
make the most beautiful pieces of art.

i'd like to be sometimes alone
to process thoughts of my own.
i'm not shutting you out
nor am i from your side about to depart.
i'm not even internally breaking apart.

silence with none but i
and the company of my thoughts
is a way to guide all my inner aspects to unify.

Grace

someday you'll find
the right amount of strength
and the necessary number
of deep breaths
to end
what's tiptoeing to its death.
with a full-stop
instead of a coma
or semi-colon for extra length.

i may look as soft
as the petals you see,
but i've grown with thorns
to reach this state of sipping tea.
it's the strength i hide behind grace and softness
that keeps me standing and not flee.
i'm made of magic, dark and light,
embedded inside of me.

sometimes it isn't about staying on the same track
but the strength to say you had enough
and move forward without looking back;
hoping that the bridges you burn
light the way ahead with no return.

questions will always rise
as we live out our life.
i'd say don't live it care-free,
nor over exaggerate the worry.
we'll learn to answer them one at a time
and once solved, we'll enjoy the victory.
and if, in the midst of an adrenaline rush
the ship began to sink and crush,
leaving you surrounded by the deepest blue,
don't allow yourself to sink so low;
an answer will swim through.

let no loss fade you away,
loss of a dream,
loss of time or a delay,
loss of your well put scheme,
or even loss of a person one day.
keep on standing with your own beam;
for even the sun's standing,
alone
but still shining.

we don't live in a world free of hurt;
we may hope not to drown in pain
but we know it'll catch us every now and then
for we're all abroad life's moving train.
we may help each other
if one were about to drown,
but we shouldn't lie to one another
in order to protect someone against a frown.
even if being honest would pain them;
dressed up lies on top of each other
won't last but end up with a frayed hem
and eventually undress to hurt worse.

if we were to be whole
and have more to our soul;
we don't have to always shine bright.
for even a day has morning and night;
we, too, have a dark side.

i'll stand by you
for the hurricane to pass.
i'll shelter you
when shards of broken glass
threaten to hurt you.
i'll walk by you through the path
you choose to follow;
together we'll get there in a flash.
but don't worry
we'll continue the half-
made journey
you were set to make;
every sacrifice is worthy
if it eases your ache.

each person we know,
we knew with a story.
but i bet the finest glory
is when somebody
walks into your territory
accidently
and stays intentionally.

we're free, to choose, more than we think we are
even when all seems impossible 'cause of how far
an emotion embedded itself within our soul;
inserted as an integral part of a surrounding whole.
but it's still our choice
what the word fear to us means;
"forget everything and run"
hide away and achieve none
of the dreamed dreams.
or "face everything and rise"
throw in a couple more tries
for dreams aren't worth not achieving
because fear's weaving
itself around our free will to choose
between the different views
of an unpleasant emotion
instead of rising into motion.

my mother surrounded me with infinite hope;
wrapping me with ribbons of love.
she filled my eyes with beauty
of everything that'll help me cope,
then stood a few steps away to watch me proudly
as i continue to live and survive the rest of the road.

on untouched shelves, after time,
one may find a collection of dust
and all this could hint to is a sign
that a build-up of actual trust
takes patience and time.

yet no matter how long it took to adjust,
built up dust and trust are only thin lines;
a swipe of a tip of a finger can thrust
them and tip a heart over.

so carefulness with a tender touch is a must
if you wish to own another person's trust.

like the sharp end of an arrow
your words pierce
through my sorrow
and unchallenged fears;
a rescue arrow that holds on
to pull me out before tomorrow
unwelcomingly appears
ready to swallow
me whole.

sometimes
it's not about having the ability
to light another's world,
but the company
to sit with them in the dark.

we may live one literal life,
but we become different versions of ourselves,
as we, like a river, flow.
valleys may bend and redirect us,
our pace may fasten or slow,
our edges may soften or harden in rush,
we may rise or dive below,
we may change with each rock we hit and brush
and our older versions, outgrow.

to love one is to go through the tough
and beautiful parts of the show.
to travel with, even if the prep's not enough
between versions through tidal bores.
to attend multiple funerals of the people they once were,
until they still, with full force.

may the heartache
you'll experience going forward
be less than the heartache
you've already endured.

he's her endless water supply
that nourishes her to blossom and grow.
she's his lighthouse,
when darkness of life consumes him; she'll glow.
he's her rock when her tears fall,
when's she's hurt, exposed and raw.
she's his backbone,
when things fall apart after a shocking blow.

this is home, this is love;
where one puts their lover above
all else to make sure their support is enough.

allow your heart to sing
a new song aside
from the heartaches and stings
you previously tried;
spread your wings
and refill your heart.

something about the way you think
feels like i could link
my thoughts to yours in sync.

to find someone
unconditionally beautiful
you aspire to become alike
is so unusual;
not for lack of beauty
but most are in refusal
to unhide.

even if you try
to solve the mystery
that is i,
you wouldn't know half my story
nor how high
my word count is
if i really began to tell the tale.

as they say
there's more to this
than meets the eye.

we'll meet halfway
to complete our growth together,
and like growing flowers sway
towards the sun;
we'll lean on each other.

no such magic as that of words.
they may take one's breath away
at first glance, as do pearls.
they might fly through to ignite
all kinds of emotions, as do birds.
some of their magic could cure
a wounded heart better than herbs.

as years go on
and a page of our calendar turns;
magic of words doesn't cease,
but continuously burns.

like a lighthouse on the far side;
words can, a drowning soul, guide.
their magic could be the reason an eye cried
or the company that held another
as their tears dried.

you might've first seen me
in the lost and found,
but i've found my ground
and now have my own sound,
thank you for sticking around.

one's light may find an easy lover;
try their hidden shade of darkness
and love them when without cover.

not all hurt people, hurt people,
not all broken people, break people,
some try to heal
and sew others back with their own needle.
for not all evil meets evil;
some don't play to be equal.

she was fearful of the night
until she discovered that light
was within her, not necessary outside.

life is not only black and white,
it's not only wrong or right;
as long as justice is drawn
then morality is achieved.
life is not only day and night,
it's not only dark or light;
otherwise we wouldn't be blessed with dawn
nor would solutions to ethical dilemmas be reached.

stars don't align
nor do skies clear;
life may not always be fine
but we could fight fear.

i may not be a painter;
but i could try to fill up your sky
with words, instead of on paper,
in hope to lighten your day.
one doesn't have to even be a writer;
words from those we love
can lift us higher
and brighter.

today shouldn't be like yesterday,
nor should tomorrow follow suit;
life's full of more fruit
than such a one-coloured sequence.

sometimes words flow
beautifully from chest to paper,
although interlaced with sorrow;
reading them could draw
and invert lips into smiles
between the deepest shades of blue.

i may like to have you with me
to encounter life and live this path,
but only because i enjoy your company
not for the goal to complete my half.

a new start can begin any time one wishes;
it's about taking ownership of a moment,
it's your life, not your opponents'.

so take action
toward the change you'd like to go through
and begin whenever suits you.

build your own home in yourself
and stack experiences on its shelves
to have a story to tell.